ANANSI'S  BIG DINNER

Based on a Folktale from Ghana

by George Bennet

NATIONAL GEOGRAPHIC LEARNING | CENGAGE Learning

One day, Anansi the spider is cooking a big dinner, but he doesn't have any yams, tomatoes, or pickles.

Anansi calls his friend Turtle for help.

yams
tomatoes
pickles

"Turtle, can you go to the store and buy these foods for me, please?" says Anansi. "Then you can eat dinner with me."

Turtle says, "Yes!"

Anansi starts cooking while Turtle goes shopping.

BEANS

Turtle comes back to Anansi's house
with some yams, a can of tomatoes,
and a big jar of pickles.
"Don't come in!" says Anansi.
"Your hands are dirty."

"I can wash my hands in the river," says Turtle.

"First, can you go to the store again?" Anansi asks. "I need some milk and a few carrots."

Anansi keeps cooking. Turtle goes shopping again.

Turtle comes back with a bottle of milk and a bunch of carrots. Anansi stops Turtle again.
"Your hands are dirty again," says Anansi.

"I can wash them," says Turtle.
"But first I need a little bread
from the store, please," says Anansi.
Anansi finishes cooking while
Turtle goes shopping again.

Turtle comes back with a loaf of bread.
Now it is late. (Turtle is very slow!)
The wonderful smells make Turtle hungry.
"Let's eat!" says Turtle.

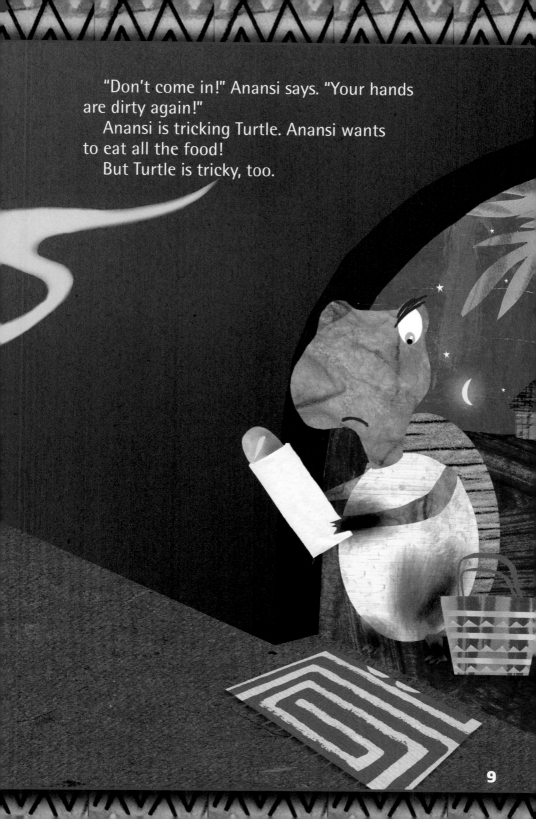

"Don't come in!" Anansi says. "Your hands are dirty again!"

Anansi is tricking Turtle. Anansi wants to eat all the food!

But Turtle is tricky, too.

"It is dark in here, Anansi. You need some light," says Turtle. "I have some candles. Here. You hold them while I light them."

Anansi holds the candles. Turtle lights them.

Now, Anansi's hands are full. He can't eat!
Turtle cleans his hands with Anansi's napkin and sits at the table.
"My hands are clean now!" says Turtle.
"Thank you, Anansi. You are a great chef!"

Facts About Recycling Cans and Bottles

Many foods and drinks come in bottles and cans. We eat the food and drink the drinks. But what happens to the cans and bottles when we are done? Old cans and bottles can be used to make other things. That is called **recycling.** Here are some things that are made from recycled cans and bottles.

Things Made from Recycled Cans

airplanes

computers

aluminum foil

Things Made from Recycled Bottles

backpacks

fleece clothes

playgrounds

In 2010, a boat made from 12,000 used bottles sailed from California to Australia. Now that's recycling!

Fun with Food

You are going to go shopping. Read the list of things you need. Circle those things in the picture. (Make sure you circle the correct number of things!)

2 bottles of milk

2 jars of pickles

4 cans of tomatoes

1 bunch of carrots

1 loaf of bread

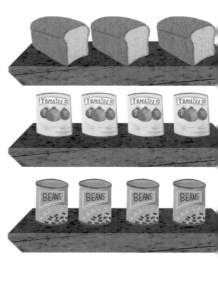

Write the words that go with each picture.

bottle of	bunch of	can of	jar of

1. a _____bottle_____ _____of_____ milk

2. a _____ _____ corn

3. a _____ _____ carrots

4. a _____ _____ pickles

Write a list of three things you can buy in cans. Write another list of three things you can buy in bottles. Use a bilingual dictionary if necessary.

Glossary

candles sticks of wax with string that are burned to make light

dirty not clean

napkin a cloth that you clean yourself with when you are eating

spider a small animal with eight legs

tricking making someone believe something that is not true

turtle an animal that lives in water and on land and has a hard shell on its back

yams sweet vegetables that look like potatoes